THE PLEASANT WAYS OF THE JEWISH DAUGHTER

Middos & Emunah

BY RABBI SHAUL WAGSCHAL

Translated from the Hebrew & adapted
by Miriam Dansky

JUDAICA PRESS, INC.

By the same author:
THE PRACTICAL HALACHA SERIES
*The Practical Guide to Kashrus; Childbirth on Shabbos;
Care of Children on Shabbos and Yom Tov;
Taharas Am Yisroel; Halochos of Aveilus;
Torah Guide for the Businessman; Laws of Interest (Ribis)*
JEWISH THOUGHT & MUSSAR
*With All Your Heart; Derech Eretz; Towards Emunah; Guide to Teshuva;
Successful Chinuch; Why I Married a Ben Torah*

ALL RIGHTS RESERVED.
NO PART OF THIS PUBLICATION MAY BE TRANSLATED,
REPRODUCED, STORED IN A RETRIEVAL SYSTEM
OR TRANSMITTED, IN ANY FORM OR BY ANY MEANS,
ELECTRONIC, MECHANICAL, PHOTOCOPYING,
RECORDING, OR OTHERWISE, WITHOUT PERMISSION
IN WRITING FROM THE PUBLISHER.

First printed 1995/5755   Reprinted 2003/5763

© Copyright 1995/5755
by Rabbi S. Wagschal
1341 47th Street, Brooklyn, NY 11219

ISBN 1-932443-03-7

Cover design by: Zisi Berkowitz

Distributed by:
THE JUDAICA PRESS, INC.
718-972-6200   800-972-6201
info@judaicapress.com • www.judaicapress.com

Distributed in Europe by:
LEHMANNS
Unit E, Viking Industrial Park
Rolling Mill Road, Jarrow
Tyne and Wear, NE32 3DP England
+44-191-430-0333   Fax: +44-191-430-0555
info@lehmanns.co.uk

Printed in Israel

CONTENTS

Preface v

CHAPTER 1
We Are Fortunate — אשרינו 1
    The Chosen People 1

CHAPTER 2
The Woman's Role in Life — תכלית האשה 4
    A Woman's Role 5
    Developing Worthy Traits 6

CHAPTER 3
***Yiras Shomayim* — יראת שמים** 8
    "The L-rd searches all hearts" 9
    Is Fear of G-d a Tangible Concept? 10

CHAPTER 4
Prayer — תפלה 12

CHAPTER 5
A Broad Look at Midos 15
    What Makes for Good Character? 15
    A Way of Self-Improvement 16

CHAPTER 6
Spiritual Happiness — שמחה 19
    Joy even at Times of Distress 20

CHAPTER 7
Truth and Falsehood — אמת ושקר 21

CHAPTER 8
Loving Kindness — חסד 23

Chapter 9

Tznius — צניעות 25
Tznius and Aristocracy 27
Tznius — Not a Jewish Invention 27

Chapter 10

Bitochon — בטחון 30
The Power of Prayer 30

Chapter 11

Orderliness 33

Chapter 12

The Torah Outlook on Health and Safety 35

Chapter 13

Reliability 38

Chapter 14

Giving Respect — דרך ארץ וכבוד הרב 40

Chapter 15

Promptness — זריזות 42
Swiftness but Not Haste 42
Causes for Slowness 43

Chapter 16

Jealousy — קנאה 45
Advice for Getting Rid of Jealousy 46

Chapter 17

Anger — כעס 48
Cure for Anger 49

Chapter 18

Pride — גאוה 51

Chapter 19
Hatred and Taking Revenge — שנאה ונקמה 53
    Taking Revenge and Bearing a Grudge 54

Chapter 20
The Evil of Arrogance 57

Chapter 21
Stinginess and Extravagance — קמצנות ופזרנות 59
    Extravagance 60
    Wasting — בל תשחית 61

Chapter 22
***Loshon Hora*, Tale-Bearing, and Refinement in Speech** 62
    Judging Others Favourably — לדון לכף זכות 62
    Curiosity 63
    Refinement in Speech 64

Chapter 23
Torah Study — לימוד תורה 65
    The Importance of *Limmud Torah* for Men 66
    The Torah Learned by Children 67
    Respect For Torah — כבוד התורה 68

Chapter 24
The Power of Repentance — תשובה 70
    The Mechanism of Repentance — תשובה 72

חלק ההלכה

Laws of *Tznius* and *Yichud*

Chapter 25
***Tznius* In Halocho** 75
    Dress 75
    Exercising in Front of Men 77
    Hair Covering 77
    Singing 78

CHAPTER 26

The Prohibition of *Yichud* 79
    With Whom 79
    Adopted Children or Stepchildren 80
    Brother and Sister 80
    The Influence of Age or State of Health 80
    Places Where *Yichud* Applies 81
    Ways in Which *Yichud* May Be Allowed 82
        The Door of The House Is Open — פתח פתוח לרשות הרבים 82
        If the Wife Is at Home — האשה בבית 82
    A Single Woman 83
    A Man and His Relatives 83

PREFACE

The last two decades have seen a quite unprecedented and explosive upsurge in the sphere of English language Judaica. New books of all descriptions and catering to all segments of the Jewish population appear on the shelves of our bookstores weekly. Nor has the youthful end of the market been overlooked. Many talented writers have expended their efforts in this direction, providing exciting and suitable literature of a Jewish character.

In adding to this plethora of literature, the author makes no apology. This book, *The Pleasant Ways of the Jewish Daughter*, is intended to be something more in the nature of a fundamental manual. It seeks to set before the Jewish girl, the basics of Torah life, which span her entire routine, both at home and at school. These are perhaps known to her in principle, but may need refreshment and reinforcement. It encompasses too, the full range of *midos tovos* and *emuno* fundamentals which she should seek to acquire and integrate into her personality.

The book is a translation of the Hebrew version דרכה בחיים which was well received in Israel. I gave full freedom to Mrs. Miriam Dansky, the translator, to adapt the book for the English reader and she has been very successful in her task.

It is my fervent wish that this *sefer* serve as an indispensable aid to the Jewish girl and woman alike.

Tammuz 5755   S. W.

CHAPTER 1

אשרינו

WE ARE FORTUNATE

אבל אנחנו עמך בני בריתך

But we are Your people, parties to Your covenant.

It is in these terms that the distinctive and elevated nature of *Bnei Yisroel* is described in the *Siddur*. Have you ever taken a moment to consider the terrific weightiness of these words — "parties to a covenant with the Almighty"? What an awesome privilege and responsibility! We say in our daily prayers:

How good is our portion, how pleasant our lot in life, how beautiful our inheritance.

Yes, it is in the final analysis a privilege to be a link in the everlasting chain of our great Jewish nation and imbued with the knowledge which is the basis of all truth, that G-d is our Master!

The Chosen People

The Torah delineates for us what our chosenness signifies:

Who can compare to this great nation, possessing fair-minded laws, such as this entire Torah?
                                                               (*Devorim* 4, 8)

We are all descendants of those who stood at *Har Sinai* and were witness to the unique event in the annals of world history, namely *Matan Torah*.

The Torah poses the following challenge concerning this stupendous event:

> *Ask of former generations, whether from the day that Heaven and Earth were created, whether on earth or to the furthermost ends of heaven, was there ever an occurrence of this magnitude? Has anything remotely resembling this ever been heard of, that the voice of G-d issued plainly from the fire and that those that heard it lived to tell the tale?*
> (*Devorim* 4, 32-33)

This indeed is the Almighty's great and eternal bequest to us, His chosen nation, and our own bequest to our children.

Observe the contrast between what we and gentiles have to offer to our children. On their side, there is nothing of eternal value — only atheistic notions, fluctuating visions and philosophies whose veracity is unfailingly disproved with the passage of time. Today, we can note this sense of bankruptcy and corruption readily in society everywhere about us.

These observations should make us feel even more keenly how fortunate we are to be the offspring of Avrohom, our forefather. He was the very first of all believers. He was courageous enough to stand in opposition to the whole world and state openly that there must be a "proprietor of the world" (as the *Midrash* expresses figuratively), a Creator and Master of Universe!

THE JEWISH DAUGHTER

Yes, we are indeed privileged to be members of this nation, whom the Almighty personally watches over. Of course, there have been many in our long history who have attempted to destroy us, yet despite all the horrendous persecutions and slaughters, the nation of Israel lives on!

We stand steadfast in our belief that the Almighty *will continue* to protect us, as He has done in the past.

The following prophecy describes the manner of our redemption.

> *If your place of exile be at the furthermost ends of the earth — from there Hashem will gather you in, take you and bring you to the land which your fathers have inherited and you shall possess it. He will do good to you and cause you to multiply in excess of your forbears.*
>
> (*Devorim* 30, 4-5)

Chapter 2

תכלית האשה

THE WOMAN'S ROLE IN LIFE

The True Purpose of Creation

We know that man was created not for his brief sojourn here in this world, but rather for his everlasting life in the next world. However, it is in this world that we are expected to prepare ourselves by performing *mitzvos* and perfecting ourselves in G-d's service, so that we may receive our reward in the World to Come. Our sages express this concept in the following manner:

> *This world resembles a corridor leading to the World to Come. Prepare yourself in the corridor, so that you may enter the room itself.*
>
> (*Ovos* 4, 21)

Physical Needs

Every individual possesses physical needs, such as the necessity to eat, drink, relax, and sleep. These do not constitute a diversion from his spiritual life but are necessary for the maintenance of good physical and mental health. Without these prerequisites man would simply be unable to serve G-d.[1]

G-d's *Mitzvos*

The six hundred and thirteen *mitzvos* prescribed in the Torah are divided into two specific categories, positive and negative. Most negative precepts apply with equal force to women as to men, for example, eating forbidden foods, keeping *Shabbos* and *Yom Tov*, forbidden speech, robbery, *Shemito*, etc.

This, however, is not true of the positive commandments which are somewhat more limited with regard to women. Women are exempt from all time-bound *mitzvos*, such as *tefillin*,[2] *tzitzis*,[3] and sitting in the *succo*. Also, the obligation of Torah study for women is not as strong as that devolving on men,[4] for reasons which we will explain shortly.

A Woman's Role

We can say in a general way, that women possess one special task in which they excel and that is to build a Jewish home and to rear generations of upright, G-d-fearing Jews. The upbringing of the children with all that this task entails is principally the responsibility of the mother.[5] It is she who is intimately connected with every aspect of child care, both physical and spiritual, as opposed to the father, the head of the household, whose involvement is much less constant and specific.

---

[1] Based up to this point on *Mesilas Yeshorim*, Chapter 1.
[2] We do not fulfill the *mitzvo* of *tefillin* on *Shabbos* or *Yom Tov*.
[3] At nighttime one is exempt from the *mitzvo* of *tzitzis*.
[4] As it is written: ולמדתם אתם את בניכם, and this has been interpreted as to exclude the daughters.
[5] As *Chazal* say: "In which merit do women get *olom habo*? By taking their children to *Cheder* (Jewish school) (*Berochos* 17).

Ezer Kenegdo

The Torah has a specific purpose in relating all the details of Chavo's creation (she being the mother of all living creatures). The Almighty clearly mapped out Odom's task in the garden of Eden — "to work and guard it."[6] These specifications indicate too, in a general sense, man's twin tasks of Torah study and the performance of positive *mitzvos* and refraining from forbidden activities. In much the same way, Chavo's task as described in the words: "I will make her a helpmate for him," symbolises the role of women, in a general sense.[7]

A woman's principle task in life is to be a helpmate to her husband (*ezer kenegdo*) and if blessed with children, a good Jewish mother. A Jewish woman acknowledges happily her role differentiation, uttering the blessing:

> *Blessed be You ... who has made me according to His will.*

Developing Worthy Traits

The perfection of one's character is an essential prerequisite for the proper observance of *mitzvos*. We can illustrate this principle clearly by drawing examples from real life. How, for example, can a girl who is always angry refrain from speaking badly of others? A jealous person will almost certainly transgress the commandment: "Do not hate your fellow-man inwardly" (*Vayikro* 14, 12).

---

[6] "To work it" — this is a positive *mitzvo*, and "to guard it" — this is a negative *mitzvo* (Rashi).

[7] It is written: "It is not good for a man to be alone" (*Bereshis* 2, 18). The *Yalkut* explains that a man without a wife is without joy, without blessing, without Torah, or peace of mind, for she complements him with all these things. But her main task is that she raises the children, and sees to all the household chores so that her husband is free to study Torah and do *mitzvos*.

THE JEWISH DAUGHTER

A habitual liar will surely stumble into the prohibition of tricking others and will fail to fulfill the *mitzvo*: "Keep your distance from a false matter" (*Shemos* 23, 7).

A Wise Person Will Be Attracted to *Mitzvos*, of His Own Accord

It is obvious that a woman who is fully occupied with the care of children will experience difficulties in observing *mitzvos* such as *tefillo*, doing acts of *chessed*, and going to *shiurim*. But any woman who finds herself in circumstances where she is not so tied down and who possesses an understanding of the immense value of *mitzvos* will not allow any opportunity for doing *mitzvos* and good deeds to elude her.

A young girl's childhood and adolescent years should form a sound basis for her life's task. In addition to acquiring the skills which she will need in her later life, e.g., proficiency in her mother tongue, communication skills, basic home economics and housewifery, a girl must take the time in these formative years to improve her character, acquire the right Torah outlook, strengthen her *emuno*, and attain a deep *yiras Shomayim*. Armed with these, she will be well equipped to withstand any external pervasive influences which she may encounter later in life.

Many girls are fortunate to receive their basic Torah training in their home, fortified by the *chinuch* efforts of the Jewish school. This alone is not enough, however. A girl needs the maturity of her later teens to consolidate and develop a true Torah outlook and a better understanding of Torah and *Halocho*. The ideal setting for this is the Seminary, with its unique atmosphere.

In summary, in her youth she must kindle an intensely blazing fire of Torah within her, which will in turn illuminate her path throughout the years ahead.

CHAPTER 3

יראת שמים

YIRAS SHOMAYIM

The key to our understanding of the difficult concept of *yiras Shomayim* can be found in Dovid *Hamelech*'s offer of guidance to his son Shlomo:

> *And now, Shlomo my son, know the G-d of your father, and serve Him with a perfect heart and a willing soul. For the L-rd searches all hearts.*
> (Divray Hayomim 1, 28, 9)

"Know G-d"

The first step towards obtaining *yiras Shomayim* is to *know* clearly that there exists a "Living G-d" Who controls the lives and fates of all living creatures.[1]

"The G-d of your father"

The second step is to recognise that this faith has been received as a tradition from our parents, grandparents, and previous

---

[1] This is the first of the thirteen principal beliefs listed by the Rambam: "I believe with perfect faith that the Creator, Blessed be He, created and controls the lives of all creatures."

generations. Furthermore, this belief is not the result of some fanciful speculation but is based on an event which was witnessed by six hundred thousand men over the age of twenty, together with their wives and children. No stories, parables, prophetic messages, or dreams formed the medium of their knowledge of the Almighty, but rather the facts of what they themselves had perceived. For G-d uttered the Ten Commandments speaking absolutely face-to-face with the whole Jewish nation,[2] as stated in the text:

> *You have been shown, to recognise that the Almighty is G-d, there is none other besides Him.*
> (*Devorim* 4, 35)

"The L-rd searches all hearts"

One of the foundations of our faith is the belief that G-d is aware not only of all of a man's actions but also of his innermost thoughts, be they good or bad. We say this in our *Rosh Hashono* prayers:

> *All secrets are revealed before You.*
> (*Musaf, Zichronos*)

It is incumbent upon us to believe too, that we are judged on our thoughts:

> *For the likeness of every creature comes before You, man's thoughts and his plans.*
> (*Musaf, Zichronos*)

This principle is true even of gentile nations who are also punished even for their bad thoughts and intentions. We find in

---

[2] The *Cuzari* writes in this way — in his first Chapter — that the Revelation at Sinai is the foundation of our belief.

connection with the slaying of the firstborn in Egypt, that even those firstborn held in prison at that time died. Rashi comments on this: "This was because they rejoiced inwardly at the plight of the Jews" (*Shemos* 12, 29), and they were punished for their evil intentions.

The importance of acquiring refinement of the heart can be demonstrated further by the fact that the Almighty struck a covenant with Avrohom our forefather, not only on the strength of his actions, but because he found his heart, his thoughts and intentions, to be pure. The text states:

> *You found his heart faithful and you entered into a covenant with Him.*
>
> (*Nechemyo* 9, 8)

Is Fear of G-d a Tangible Concept?

We know that the Almighty sees but is not seen, and it is therefore extremely difficult for us to understand the concept of "fear of G-d" in a tangible way. Reb Yochanan was aware of the intrinsic difficulty that this concept poses for the vast majority of people. In this context, he offered his pupils the following piece of advice:

> *Let the fear of Heaven be upon you as strongly as the fear of flesh and blood.*
>
> (*Berochos* 28)

"How can this be?" they exclaimed. "No more fear than that accorded to flesh and blood?" He replied, "I wish with all my heart that you would fear the Almighty even to that degree."

On reflection, we find that Reb Yochanan's words strike home. We know for example that a person is always more likely to commit a transgression or offence secretly — despite the knowledge that the Almighty sees his deeds. However, a person's intense feelings of shame would cause him to ponder long and deeply before committing this same act in front of another person.

It would be good practice for a young girl, before embarking on a certain course of action, to consider whether this is something she would willingly do in front of her friends, parents, or teachers. One classical example of this is the case of Yosef *Hatzaddik* who saved himself from Potiphar's wife's enticements by conjuring up the image of his saintly father, Yaakov *Ovinu*.[3]

Sayings of Our Sages

> *You will in the future be required to give a reckoning in front of the King of Kings, the Almighty One, Blessed be He.*
>
> (*Ovos* 4, 29)

> *Know what is above you — a seeing eye, a listening ear, and that all your deeds are inscribed in a book.*
>
> (*Ovos* 2, 1)

---

[3] Rashi writes that Yosef saw a vision of his father's face.

CHAPTER 4

תפלה

PRAYER

The way in which we pray is modelled on two great women of old — Leoh *Immenu* and Channo, wife of Elkono. What was Leoh's innovation? We are told that she was the first individual in the annals of world history to express openly her feelings of thankfulness to the Almighty. Up to this point, individuals acknowledged the fact that *Hashem* controls all events, in their use of the term *Boruch*,[1] and this was felt to be sufficient. Leoh's words, however, implied that this is not enough! One's heart must be actively stimulated to express praise and thanksgiving to the Almighty. In this vein, Dovid *Hamelech* states:

> *My heart and flesh shall praise the living G-d.*
> (*Tehillim* 84, 3)

Channo's contribution was the manner of prayer, which we still use today. She demonstrated that the locality in which prayer takes place is the heart. Her prayer was silent:

---

[1] Eliezer, the servant of Avrohom, said this: ברוך ה' אלקי אדוני אברהם וכו' (בראשית כ"ד,כ"ז). "Blessed be G-d, the master of Avrohom." In the same way Shem, the son of Noach, said: וברוך קל עליון וכו' (בראשית י"ד,כ'). "And blessed is the Almighty G-d, etc."

> *Her lips were moving but her voice was not heard.*
> (*Shmuel 1*, 1, 13)

Her words were not enunciated loudly, but represented an inward dialogue.[2]

In yet another area of prayer, we take the lead from two women. This is the format for proclaiming *Shiro* for which the Song of Devoro[3] and the thanksgiving prayer of Channo on the birth of her son, Shmuel *Hanovi*, act as blueprints.[4]

Women, it would seem, have a special sensitivity in prayer. In fact, we know that the ultimate redemption will ensue in the merit of a woman's tears:

> *A voice is heard in the heights of Heaven, the sound of bitter weeping. It is Rochel, who weeps for her children... Withhold your voice from weeping, and your eyes from tears, for there is a reward for your toil, said the L-rd. You shall return from your enemy's land. There is hope for your end, says the L-rd. Your children shall return to their border.*
> (*Yirmeyohu* 31, 14-17)

---

[2] The *Gemoro* (*Berochos*) derives it from the text: *Only her lips were moving* — "From these words we derive the lesson that one who prays must move his lips." *And her voice was not heard* — "From this we learn that it is forbidden to raise one's voice in prayer." *And behold she spoke from her heart* — "From this we derive the lesson that one who prays must have accompanying sincere feelings."

[3] *Shoftim*. Chapter 5. Also on *Krias Yam Suf*: "And Miriam the Prophetess, the sister of Aharon, took the cymbal in her hand. And all the women followed her with cymbals and dances. And Miriam said to them: 'Sing to the L-rd, for He is highly exalted. The horse and his rider, He has drowned in the sea'" (*Shemos* 15, 2-21).

[4] *Shmuel 1*, 2, 1-10, a reference to the whole prayer.

In the area of prayer, it is quality and not quantity which is crucial. Even lack of knowledge of Hebrew does not provide a barrier; prayer can be expressed in any vernacular. Sincerity is the yardstick and not length of prayer. We know that the simplest of sacrifices offered by the poor man is just as acceptable to G-d as the greatest of a wealthy man.

Do not become despondent therefore if you are a girl or married woman with very little time to pray. Even one chapter of *Tehillim* or any other short prayer is precious in G-d's eyes. In times of true distress, a few short words such as: "*Hashem*, please help me," uttered with heartfelt intention, have the power to pierce Heaven![5]

> *Hashem is near to all who call on Him with sincerity.*
> (*Tehillim* 145, 18)

> *Pour out your heart like water before the L-rd.*
> (*Eicho* 2, 19)

> *Save me, O L-rd, for the waters threaten my life.*
> (*Tehillim* 69, 2)

> *Pour out your hearts before Him, G-d be a stronghold to us, Selah.*
>
> (*Tehillim* 62, 9)

---

[5] We find in this context, that at a time of need, Moshe kept his prayer to a minimum, and he said just the following: "Please G-d, heal her (Miriam)" (*Bemidbar* 12, 13).

CHAPTER 5

מדות טובות

A BROAD LOOK AT MIDOS

What Makes for Good Character?

Man is a complex bundle of desires. These desires hold sway over him and from morning till night he tries to satisfy them. He desires to eat or to drink; he wishes to sleep; he experiences an urge to hear the latest news or to see what is happening on the street. We must not, however, generalise by stating that all desires are inherently bad. A person must be motivated, for example, to look after his physical needs. Without food, drink, or rest he simply could not function. But desires and feelings that do not fall within this category are designated *midos*. These can be good or bad and are controlled by the intellect. The problems arise only because one's intellect or rationale is open to enticement. The solution is to fortify one's intellect. If one is profoundly aware of the truth at all times, no perversions of judgment will deflect one from the right course.

Human beings possess worthy characteristics too, such as mercifulness and the desire to perform kind acts. It is to these noble sides of his character that a person should veer, whilst simultaneously seeking to distance himself from his bad *midos*. In this manner, one will achieve a general improvement of character.[1]

A Person's Individuality

Each person is born with his or her individualised set of *midos*. These cover a vast range of qualities. There are those who are inclined to anger, and conversely, those who are too easy-going. Yet again there are those who are naturally kind and generous, and those who are stingy by inclination. There are some who are proud, yet others who are humble. All these traits are actually present in every individual; it is just the exact balance and amalgam which differs from person to person.[2] We all have varying raw materials with which to work, but we are all required to strive, in our different ways, for perfection of character.[3]

A Way of Self-Improvement

A useful tool for self-improvement lies in the power of repetitive actions. Someone who has done a particular action three or four times will find it far easier to perform the same action in the future. It is a good idea to set oneself easy tasks to accomplish in this sphere. Success in more difficult areas will soon follow. This principle is well illustrated by the classic example of Rabbi Akiva. The *Gemoro* tells us that he was forty years old and had never learned a word of Torah. One day he was standing by a well and noticed the formation of a certain stone. "Who sculpted this stone?" he asked bystanders. "Nobody," was the reply. "It is shaped by the water which falls on it steadily, every day." He was

---

[1] Every time a person controls his base qualities, he refines them a little.
[2] According to the Rambam in *Hilchos Deos*, Chapter 1.
[3] Therefore there is no need for pride, in one whose *midos* are noble (without any particular effort), for thus one was born. Similarly, one who suffers from bad characteristics is not essentially bad, or worse than one's friends (according to Divine reckoning), because these qualities have been allotted to one by G-d.

greatly astonished by this. They said to him, "Akiva, have you never read the verse: 'Stones that were sculpted by water'?" (*Iyov* 14, 19). Immediately, Akiva applied it to his own situation, thinking to himself: "If water, a soft substance, wore away at stone, the hardest of substances, how much more so might the words of Torah, which are strong as iron, mould my own person which is comprised only of soft flesh and blood!" Immediately he began to study Torah. (*Ovos deRebbe Nosson,* Chap. 10, 2)

The same principle applies to *midos* correction. Every good action makes an impression on an individual, and if performed often enough will in the course of time refine and transform a person's character.

Character Perfection — Step-by-Step

Any girl attempting to improve herself and eradicate unworthy qualities should not begin with extreme measures. Rather she should set herself aims which she thinks she can achieve.

One's motto should be: "Better to aim lower but fulfill one's intentions than attempt too much and be unable to carry it through."

All Beginnings Are Hard

To behave in a changed way requires effort, but it will prove less challenging as time goes on. As has been said, accustom yourself firstly to easy actions. If you find you cannot fulfill everything you set out to do, build up gradually. But how do we define easy tasks in terms of character-building? Here are two examples. Inquire how your friends are, with a pleasant expression, or carry out small acts of kindness. These are the types of actions which lie within your grasp, and you will not have to suffer much internal opposition in fulfilling them. Later on, progress to more difficult goals. For example: not getting into a temper, or not allowing oneself to become jealous or resentful. These are more difficult issues simply because they are entirely governed by one's emotions.[4]

If you find that you have set yourself too unrealistic aims, do a little less. But what you certainly should *not* do is say: "I will leave everything as it is for the time being and work on my *midos* at a later date." For if you leave off altogether, you will lose everything. Remember the following maxim: One never wins a war (at one attempt); one wins a battle.

---

[4] This method of correcting *midos* is based on *Sefer Hayoshor* by *Rabbenu Tam*.

CHAPTER 6

שמחה

SPIRITUAL HAPPINESS

Spiritual happiness, which is the only true happiness, can be acquired only through faith. For only someone who truly believes in the controlling Hand of the Almighty can be completely at peace with him- or herself. Our Sages remark, "Who is rich? He who rejoices in his lot." Nor will worries about the future control his outlook, for he will always feel that the Almighty will "do what is good in His eyes."

This type of inner peacefulness has many tangible benefits:

(1) Feeling joyful at all times actually prevents many physical illnesses and ailments.[1]

(2) Any action carried out in a joyful manner will be accomplished easily and speedily. What a person can achieve in one hour of joyful work will be impossible to carry out in the course of many hours of work carried out in a depressed manner.

---

[1] This is widely accepted in the medical world.

(3) A happy person will have many friends. He or she will be universally loved for his or her cheerful, smiling countenance.

Serve *Hashem* With Joy

The service of G-d should also be enacted in a joyful manner, but with a special type of joy which contains within it elements of fear.[2] We should experience a deep and abiding sense of joy and inner satisfaction, at being part of the chosen nation, which is dedicated to G-d's service, as stated in the text:

> *And you shall be a treasure to Me from all the nations.*
>
> (*Shemos* 19, 5)

Yet simultaneously we ought to feel fear at approaching a great and awesome King.

Joy Even at Times of Distress

Our subtitle would appear to be self-contradictory. The truth is that once we acknowledge that *everything* — all occurrences, whether good or bad — emanates from the Almighty, this will lead us automatically to a joyful acceptance of all situations. We will understand that they must be for *our* good, even if we fail to see this with our limited perspective.

Our Sages stated, "A person is duty bound to offer blessings for the bad ('Blessed be the true Judge') in the same way as he utters a blessing for the good ('Blessed be He Who is good and bestows good')." The words "in the same way" have been interpreted by the *Gemoro* to mean that concerning both occurrences, one must give thanks with a perfectly happy heart.

---

[2] It is written in *Tehillim*: "Rejoice in trembling" (*Tehillim* 2, 11). This means that joy and rejoicing should be mixed with trembling.

CHAPTER 7

אמת ושקר

TRUTH AND FALSEHOOD

It is hard to understand in a purely rational way, how people can stoop to lying and falsehood. After all, every person possesses an intellect which should tell him clearly what is honest and what is dishonest. It is an especially surprising quality if found in Jews, who traditionally excel in truthfulness:[1]

> *The remnant of Israel do not speak falsely, nor is there any deceitfulness to be found in their speech.*
> (*Zephanyo* 3, 13)

Rabbi Moshe Luzato (in *Mesilas Yeshorim*, Chapter 11) writes that strangely enough, there are those who impose many stringencies on themselves in other areas, but neglect matters concerning falsehood and deceit. Furthermore, our Rabbis have revealed to us that most of the world "are guilty of robbery." The *Mesilas Yeshorim* explains that this is not meant literally but refers to the common propensity to find excuses where profit is involved. It is for this very reason that complete truthfulness in *all* areas of

---

[1] The seal of G-d is truth, and the soul is the Divine part of man, therefore truthfulness is characteristic of the soul.

life is not widespread. It is therefore up to the individual and his own conscience to ensure that the negative influences of the environment do not alter his judgement in this respect. The text states:

> *Do not incline after the majority for misdeed.*
> *(Shemos 23, 2)*

What Is Not True — is False!

It is forbidden to tell a lie even if one derives no benefit from it at all. For example, a girl relates an incident which has occurred or repeats a conversation. In the course of transmitting information, she changes general details, as the mood takes her. This is forbidden. Again, if she has heard a certain item of news, and before making sure whether it is true of false, she proceeds to relate it to others — this would not be permitted.[2]

Falsifying and How It Relates to One's Service of G-d

Someone who is prepared to lie and falsify cannot serve G-d properly. For such a girl will try constantly to justify her false values to her friends and she will also attempt to compensate for her distorted judgement on a spiritual plane.

---

[2] וכך הוא במס׳ דרך ארץ זוטא פרק א׳: אהוב את השמא ושנא את המה בכך.

CHAPTER 8

LOVING KINDNESS

Tell us, man, what is good and what G-d seeks from you — other than to perform justice and to love doing kindnesses.

(*Micho* 6, 8)

These words of the prophet teach us that far from kindness being a noble quality which only elevated individuals are expected to have, it is one of the most basic qualities which G-d seeks from every one of us.

Nor is a mechanical performance of good deeds good enough; rather we are told to let the *love* of kindness permeate our hearts. This is what the prophet stresses.[1]

It is questionable whether a girl who performs a kind action, only after she has been begged to do so two or three times by her friends and is unable to refuse their requests, is accredited with this action. Certainly, her deeds cannot be included in the category of "love of kindness."

---

[1] Based on *Chofetz Chaim* in his *sefer Ahavas Chessed*, Part 2, Chapter 1.

Deeds without Measure!

Loving kindness is infinite — it cannot set limits.[2] The concept "I have done enough" can never apply here. (But it is permissible to say, "I have done everything that is in my power to do.") Our Sages explain the words "You should surely give" (*Devorim* 15, 10) to mean to give even one hundred times to the same person.[3]

Just as there is no maximum limit on kindness, there is no minimum limit. Even the smallest act has its importance and is worthwhile doing.[4]

What constitutes kindness to others? With regard to girls in particular, there are many actions one might try to do: helping a friend with her homework (if she finds it difficult to do it alone), picking up something at the shops either for friends or family members, visiting the sick,[5] comforting those who are grieving, encouraging those who are feeling low, making friends with new neighbours. In some of these cases a few well-chosen warm words and a pleasant face will be enough to raise one's fellow-creature's spirits. This is after all the central goal of one's efforts of *chessed*.

---

[2] As we say in the *berochos* that we recite over the Torah: אלו דברים שאין להם שעור...וגמילות חסדים...
[3] Quoted in Rashi, *Devorim* 15, 10.
[4] The main purpose of *chessed* is the satisfaction and pleasure that one brings to one's fellow-man and there is no difference essentially, in which way one causes this pleasure to be derived — whether through a big or small deed.
[5] We are told that R. Akiva visited his sick pupil, and because he cleared and swept his room, his pupil said to him: "Rebbe, you have revived me" (*Nedorim* 40).

CHAPTER 9

צניעות

TZNIUS

What Is *Tznius*?

Tznius is an all-embracing concept which is difficult to define in exact terms. Certainly one can say that *tznius* is one of the main methods through which an individual acquires refinement and a measure of self-dignity.

The term *tznius* comes from the Hebrew root which means "hidden" or "sheltered". The whole point of *tznius* is that a girl or a woman should behave in such a way as to suggest that she shuns publicity, that she sees but is not seen.[1] When she walks on the street her resolve should be "I do not want to attract attention."[2] This is the true basis of *tznius* and all else flows naturally from this concept. A truly modest woman feels no sense of denial or frustration at having to follow the dictates of the Torah in this

---

[1] For she is like a princess — and all the princess's glory is within. This is a woman's strong point, as we read in *Yalkut Vayero* on the *possuk*: "Where is Sarah, your wife?"

[2] On the subject of Dino, the daughter of Yaakov, our Rabbis asked, "What caused her to fall into the snare of Shechem? Because *she went out* — as the *possuk* says: ותצא דינה."

sphere.³ Nor will she allow a misplaced expression of *tznius* to prevent her from sometimes acting in ways which are obviously removed from *tznius*, in accordance with the needs of the moment!⁴

Tznius in Practical Manifestations

Tznius is demonstrated in the following ways:

(1) One's way of walking — This should be quiet and unobtrusive, without any attraction-seeking mannerisms (perhaps looking downwards, in the manner of modest women).

(2) Clothing — Clothes should be of modest cut and refined colours. (See Chapter 25, page 75)

(3) Speech — One should adopt a quiet tone, with a refined choice of expressions.

(4) Conduct — This should be modest but at the same time pleasant.

---

³ *Rabbenu Yona* writes in his *Igeres Teshuvo*: A woman must be modest, and take care that men other than her husband do not look at her, for she may cause them to sin.
Even between husband and wife there is a place for modesty, as Rashi explains in *Bereshis* 12, 11, that Avrohom had never truly recognised Soroh's great beauty due to the modesty that existed between them.

⁴ It is written in *Yalkut, Bemidbar* 27: "In that generation the women repaired what the men breached." Aharon said: "Take off your golden nose rings" (to make the golden calf) but the women did not wish to do so, and they opposed their husbands. The men did not want to enter the holy land but the women (the daughters of Tzlofchod) asked for their portion of Eretz Yisroel.
We learn in *Yalkut, Shoftim* 84, that the husband of *Devoro* was an ignoramus. She said to him, "Come, I will make wicks and you go and bring them to the *Bais Hamikdosh*." She made the wicks especially thick so that they would give out a lot of light. G-d, who knows the thoughts of men, said to her, "You had the intention of increasing My light — I will surely cause your light to shine in Judah and Israel."

THE JEWISH DAUGHTER

These categories cover all aspects of the standards of general behaviour for girls and married women alike.

Tznius and Aristocracy

Tznius is highly becoming to a woman, and indeed enhances her innate femininity. We say this, despite modern tendencies to downgrade the natural sense of *tznius* in women, and the subsequent sweeping away of all barriers of reserve and shame in society at large.

A married woman imbued with *tznius* dresses smartly with one thought paramount in her mind — to please her husband. Yet she does not allow her standards of modesty to fall when she is outside her own house. Even going into the street should be viewed by her as an unavoidable infringement on the aristocratic status of the Jewish woman, especially nowadays, as society at large has relinquished all notions and standards of decency.

Any girl or woman who works outside the home must pay particular attention to *tznius*. Her desire to make a good impression at work should never lead her to compromise on these Torah-given standards.

Tznius — Not a Jewish Invention

Tznius, as such, is not a concept which is confined to the Jewish nation. In fact, when we look at photographs or pictures of bygone eras we are immediately impressed by the general level of modesty. Sadly, this is no longer so nowadays and the deterioration in moral standards can be traced directly to a general loss of faith in G-d. Believing that man is descended from the ape is certainly not conducive to maintaining high standards of moral conduct. Unfortunately, these general trends have had their pervasive effect on Jews too, and even on the Orthodox section.

Our position on these matters should however be diametrically opposed to the general consensus of opinion, knowing as we do that there is a Creator, and possessing the Torah which governs our daily behaviour.

The Torah also informs us that Chavo was created for a particular task, as is explained in the *Yalkut*:

> G-d did not create the woman from the head of Odom, so that she would not be light-headed; nor from the eye, so that she would not be inquisitive; nor from the ear, so that she would not be an eavesdropper; nor from the hand, so that she would not be acquisitive; nor from the foot, so that she would not be one who seeks publicity. Rather, she was formed from a hidden part of man's body, from a rib. Whilst creating each limb, He said to her, "Be a modest woman."

This *Yalkut* demonstrates that *tznius* is a woman's most central characteristic!

Tznius in the Home

Tznius a natural sense of shame, should not be confined to the public arena, but should be adhered to even in private. For example, even when alone in the house a woman should not reveal parts of her body which are normally concealed, if there is no pressing need to do so. This should accrue not only from her natural modesty, but also from her awareness that the Almighty sees all our deeds, at all times.[5]

◄◄❖►►

---

[5] The *Gemoro* tells us about Kimchis, who said that she merited to have seven sons, High Priests, because she never uncovered her hair, even in the privacy of her own four walls. (This is related too about the mother of the Chazon Ish.)

CHAPTER 10

בטחון

BITOCHON

Bitochon is not just a belief in G-d as the Creator of the Universe; it is a firm knowledge that the Almighty guides us at all times. Prayer is our link to this All-seeing G-d, who can fulfill all our requests. G-d watches over us at all times with loving care and mercifulness and it is a fundamental cornerstone of our faith that all that befalls us in life, is for our ultimate good. We must believe this even if we do not always understand how this can be so.

Armed with this strong belief, all worry about the future should be banished from our hearts.

The Power of Prayer

G-d desires that we pray for all our needs. If, however, our prayers are not immediately fulfilled, we should not despair of mercy.[1] This was the method employed by our forefathers, whose deeds we are urged to emulate. For example, Yitzchok, our forefather, prayed for a child for many years and his request was finally fulfilled after a period of twenty years.

---

[1] Thus, we are told by the *Gemoro* that he who prays and is not answered should pray again. As it is said: "Trust in the L-rd" — and if you are not answered — "Fortify your heart and trust in the L-rd" (*Berochos* 32).

THE JEWISH DAUGHTER

A Word of Warning

It is foolish to think that G-d will grant all a believer's requests automatically. However, it is also a principle of our faith that *Hashem* can help us when to all appearance, there seems to be no hope at all. If solutions which accord with one's individual desires are not forthcoming, one must believe that this is the will of G-d and accept this gracefully.[2]

This concept is further expounded on by *Rabbenu Tam* in *Sefer Hayoshor*. He explains that when we experience times of tranquillity in our life, we ought to feel that this pleasant state is not guaranteed. One should always be in a state of mental readiness to accept the Almighty's decrees — whatever they might be. Thus, no loss of faith will incur should misfortune strike. Truly, all human beings are like vessels in the hand of the potter, who either holds it up or breaks it, at will. We might feel less bitter too, if we remember that what seems bad at a certain moment in time might, in reality, not be so. The *Yalkut* also cites many anecdotes illustrating this point, one of which we quote here. A story is told concerning two men who intended to go on a business trip. One was injured when he stepped on a thistle, and was unable to board the ship. Understandably, he was extremely upset at being prevented from undertaking his journey. Several days later, he heard that the ship on which his friend had sailed had sunk without survivors. He began to offer thanksgiving and praise to G-d. This story illustrates the true meaning of the prophet's words:

> *I will thank G-d for You have rejected me — may You return to comfort me.*
>
> (*Yeshayohu* 12, 1)

---

[2] According to R. Avrohom the son of the Rambam, in his work, *Hamaspik Leovdei Hashem*, Chapter on *Bitochon*.

A story is told concerning Rabbi Akiva, who used to say; a person should always accustom himself to say: "Everything that G-d causes to happen is ultimately for the good." The *Gemoro* relates that one day R. Akiva was travelling and he entered a certain city, but he could not find a roof for the night. He therefore bedded down in a field, and he had an ass and a hen and a lamp. A wind blew up and extinguished his lamp, a cat came and killed his hen, and a lion came and ate his ass. As each thing happened, he proclaimed: "Everything that *Hashem* has done is good." That night, a band of robbers attacked the town, capturing all the inhabitants — and he alone escaped. And because his lamp was extinguished and neither his ass nor his hen could make a sound, the robbers never realised his whereabouts.[3]

Quotations about Bitochon

Trust in G-d — strengthen your heart and trust in G-d.

(*Tehillim* 27, 14)

Thrust your burden on Him and He will sustain you.

(*Tehillim* 55, 23)

Trust in G-d with all your heart and do not rely on your own intelligence.

(*Mishlei* 3, 5)

My eyes are continually on the L-rd, for He will free my feet from the snare.

(*Tehillim* 25, 15)

✧

---

[3] *Berochos* 60.

Chapter 11

ORDERLINESS

We might ask ourselves: Does orderliness come under the category of good *middos*, or is it simply a generally worthwhile quality?

Rabbi Yisroel Salanter comments that orderliness is a highly praiseworthy trait, the lack of which implies a certain deficiency in one's service of G-d. This is because disorderliness in one's day-to-day affairs reflects a certain *spiritual slovenliness*. Such an individual's outlook on life will be confused and hazy and he will find difficulty in articulating any clearly formulated ideas.

How do we accustom ourselves to being *orderly* in our service of *Hashem*? The *Mesilas Yeshorim* tells us that the correction of character can be accomplished only through actions because actions influence one's state of mind.[1]

By striving to work and behave in an orderly manner we will influence our approach to *avodas Hashem*. One could start with this simple exercise: Assign each object or book to a special place and make sure we return it each time we use it.

---

[1] See end of Chapter 5 and the beginning of Chapter 23.

In this vein, we may quote the example of a certain *godol* who owned a vast library. He was so particular about returning each book to its proper place, that he was easily able to lay his hand on any *sefer* he needed, even in the dark.

Actually, orderliness benefits not just those around one, but principally the individual herself. Anyone who has wasted time looking for misplaced objects will readily attest to the truth of this statement.

In answer to the question raised at the beginning of this chapter, we might say that orderliness is a good quality which has immense practical value and also promotes spiritual harmony.

≪❖≫

Chapter 12

THE TORAH OUTLOOK ON HEALTH AND SAFETY

You should guard your lives very carefully.
(Devorim 4, 15)

From this text we derive the following guidelines:

(a) A girl must guard her health carefully and not endanger herself in any way. Anyone who enters willingly into potentially life-threatening situations obviously does not place a proper value on her life. In other cultures, it is considered prestigious to engage in dangerous pursuits, such as journeys to remote regions or climbing mountains. In the Torah tradition, however this is viewed as a lack of moral seriousness. For our view is that the soul is joined to the body with a particular end in mind, namely the service of G-d. One's body is only on loan; and one is dutybound to guard an object on loan with special care.[1]

---

[1] This is what the Rambam says in *Hilchos Deos*, Chapter 4: "It is necessary for the body to be healthy, for the service of G-d, for it is impossible to understand the ways of the Creator if one is ill. Therefore, an individual is duty bound to distance himself

(b) What has been said about physical health applies with even greater force to moral health. A person should always attempt to distance himself from morally-testing situations, and thereby avoid stumbling into transgression.

The main way we can achieve this end is to keep away from places which might test our self-control. For as long as we remain aloof from the *yetzer hora* we can still maintain some control over our deeds. But should we stray into a sinful vicinity, our *yetzer hora* immediately begins to gain dominance. This is why we pray daily: "Do not bring us into the proximity of sin."

This category includes many varieties of activity, including keeping bad company and reading books and newspapers which both arouse the evil inclination and propagate false outlooks.

Taking Care Not to Frequent Dark or Lonely Places

Unfortunately, in every day and age there are certain individuals whose sole purpose in life is to gratify their own lusts. Such people might approach one with a convincing act of being concerned for one's welfare. The only precaution one can take is *always* to stay away from lonely places or deserted streets (even in city centres) and parks or secluded country walks, especially at night.

One must be aware that this danger applies not only outside the house but inside it too. A girl should never let a strange man in to the house (even if he be a Jew who *looks* reliable) when she is alone. In this respect, one should heed the advice of our Sages:

---

from matters which endanger the health of the body, and to accustom himself to healthy habits and pursuits.

It is therefore forbidden to walk next to a crumbling wall, or any unsafe place. One of the duties of a father is to teach his children to swim (*Kidushin* 29).

"Honour him but suspect him!" This stricture applies equally to single girls or married women. And one must surely never enter a strange man's abode — unless one knows for certain that other grown-up family members are inside.

≪❖≫

CHAPTER 13

RELIABILITY

We can observe that in our daily lives we are dependent on many individuals. Children are dependent on the driver who brings them to school, adults on bakers for bread, grocers and shopkeepers who provide goods on a daily basis, on companies who supply the needs of the community such as heating, gas, and water. This principle applies also to families or schools where each individual is dependent on the other in a variety of ways. In the family unit, for example, the father is responsible for providing the livelihood, the mother for food preparation, and the daughter helps the mother and so on.

Every girl should try to train herself in reliability. She should help in the house willingly and be aware that if she fails in her duties, she is letting down those around her.

Let us imagine the following situation: A girl is at her friend's house. She receives a phone call from her mother asking her to stop at the grocery shop on her way home to buy two loaves of bread. He mother warns her: "Don't forget — I have nothing else in the house for supper." "Sure, Mummy. You can rely on me," the girl says glibly. By the time she leaves her friend's house, she has already forgotten altogether about the grocery shop and the bread. And when she gets home, she has to go all the way back to the shop to find it is already shut. We can well imagine the crisis in the house that evening.

Letting Someone Know That the Errand Asked for Has Been Done

It is common decency to inform someone who asked you to do something that it has been done. Incidentally, this applies with greater force if it has *not* been done! Partly, this constitutes an act of kindness and respect towards the one who has made the request. It will alleviate unnecessary worry about whether the errand has been fulfilled or not and it therefore shows a commendable sense of concern for the feelings of others.

⋘❖⋙

CHAPTER 14

דרך ארץ וכבוד הרב

GIVING RESPECT

Rise before an old man and give respect to the elderly.

(*Vayikro* 19, 32)

The second part of this verse teaches us that it is not enough simply to stand up for an old man or a *Talmid Chochom*, but that we are duty bound to accord him *honour* in a multitude of other ways.

Our *Rishonim* teach us that each of the Ten Commandments serves as a central principle to other *mitzvos* contained in the Torah, which resemble this fundamental pronouncement in type.[1] For example, "Remember the Sabbath Day to keep it holy" serves as the basis for the prohibition of *melocho* on *Yomim Tovim* too. In the same way, the *mitzvo* of honouring one's parents serves as the bedrock for a number of allied concepts, e.g., giving respect to

---

[1] Rashi comments in *Parshas Yisro* (Chapter 14, 12) that all the 613 *mitzvos* are included in the *Aseres Hadibros*.

elderly people, *Rabbonim*, *Talmidai Chachomim*, teachers, elder brothers, grandparents, aunts and uncles.[2]

The minimum amount of *kovod* that one should accord parents is to behave in a respectful manner towards them. This means not speaking to them in the same way as to a friend and obviously not being insolent to them.

Generally speaking, *kibud ov vo'aim* compels us not to contradict our parents even on matters on which we are knowledgeable, nor to reinforce their opinions by saying, "Daddy (or Mummy), *you* are right!"

The details of *kibud ov vo'aim* are truly a subject on their own, and we have merely touched on them in this context.

---

[2] For a full treatment of the subject of *Derech Eretz*, see *Guide to Derech Eretz* by the same author.

Chapter 15

זריזות

PROMPTNESS

The quality of *zerizus* (swiftness) is very highly praised as a tool in serving G-d and also brings success to an individual in his day-to-day dealings.

Swiftness but Not Haste

All of a person's actions require preparation and planning. Thus, although speed is a wonderful quality, haste is not! There is a saying: "Regret is the fruit of haste." So before carrying out any action, weigh up in your mind: should you do it, and how? Once you have decided to do it and how to do it, carry it out as a matter of urgency!

Zerizus in Practice

(1) When the chance comes to do a *mitzvo* or another worthy act — do it straight away, for unnecessary delay might lead one to eventual non-fulfillment. This principle is *well-tried and tested*. Our Sages note, "Do not defer a *mitzvo* that comes your way."

THE JEWISH DAUGHTER

(2) In fulfilling the *mitzvo* or other act, do it in a speedy manner. We see this in the case of Rivko, where the text states, "And she hurried and lowered the pitcher," and again, "she hurried," and "she ran to the well" (*Bereshis* 24, 18-20).[1] *Chazal* remark concerning her that: "The actions of the righteous are all done quickly."[2] Even in the trivial act of lowering the pitcher from the shoulder to the arm, we recognise the difference between one who acts with due promptness and one who does not.

Causes for Slowness

There are some girls who do everything at a slow pace, and they find difficulty in completing all the work which they are given. There are several possible causes for this:

(1) Lack of concentration on the job itself. Some girls daydream in time allotted for work.

(2) Letting their wish to produce *perfect-looking* work override all other considerations.

(3) Fear that they may not be able to accomplish the task, and therefore, doing it slowly — thinking about each step two or three times.

It is very difficult to change anyone's nature overnight — and such a girl will need to consult experienced people for advice on her particular problem.

---

[1] Up to this point, based on *Mesilas Yeshorim* (*Perek* 6-8).
[2] Quoted in *Mesilas Yeshorim*, Chapter 7, in the name of the *Midrash Rabbo, Bemidbar, Parsho* 10.

She might also ponder the following thought: Is it worthwhile my spending so much time on one aspect of my work if I will not be able to achieve a proper and complete outcome?

Laziness

The greatest impediment to speed is *laziness*. By inclination, people do not like hard work. However, we can observe that when a person really and truly desires a certain outcome, all obstacles magically disappear! Laziness too is swept away, for the object of his or her desire is so precious, that all efforts needed to accomplish it are trifling in his or her eyes.

A study of this character trait will reveal that by and large, phrases such as "I cannot do it" really mean "I do not want to do it," and that "It is too hard" means "It doesn't interest me." However, the lazy individual seldom recognises his or her excuses for what they are, for the uppermost thought in his or her mind is self-justification.

❖

CHAPTER 16

קנאה

JEALOUSY

Jealousy is a chronic illness which afflicts the majority of mankind at one time or other. Jealousy can be focused on the higher social status, career achievements, or material possessions of another individual.

Jealousy is such a strong emotion that it is instantly recognisable even externally, on one's facial features. (There is a well-known idiom which expresses this truth: "green with envy.")

The *Mesilas Yeshorim* writes on this subject: "Jealousy is truly an idiotic emotion — for by being jealous one gains nothing nor does one necessarily harm the one against whom this emotion is directed. Truly, the one who is harmed the most is the individual himself, for jealousy prevents one from appreciating all the benefits one already possesses."

There are also those who hover on the borderline of jealousy. They may become discontented if they see those outside their immediate family circle getting on better than they are. Although they enunciate expressions of joy on so-and-so's good fortune, inside they feel some form of resentment. This feeling is not defined as *true jealousy* but it does contain elements of it.

Advice for Getting Rid of Jealousy

Our principle advice to a jealous girl is to remind her that she will not benefit at all from being jealous and that on the contrary, she might derive much aggravation. She should ask herself: "Do I really need this pain?"

Another piece of advice in combating jealousy is to stop comparing one's situation with that of others. We are duty bound to believe that everything is under the Almighty's close supervision even if we cannot understand the manner in which material goods or other benefits are distributed!

'Good' Jealousy

Even though jealousy is, generally speaking, a bad trait, there are times when its exercise can be beneficial. That is when it is directed towards the *yiras Shomayim* or good deeds of another. Our Sages teach us that "the jealousy of (another) learned man increases wisdom." If one sees one's friend performing a certain good deed or *mitzvo*, one should try to attain one's friend's level by saying: "If he can do it, so can I."

We find this principle illustrated in connection with Avrohom our forefather who asked Shem the son of Noach in what merit they had been privileged to leave the ark after the flood. This was Shem's answer:

> *"We merited to leave the ark because of the kindness we showed to the animals and the birds. We did not sleep — but we put out their food and*

> *drink (for it is well-known that there are certain animals who only eat at night)."* Hearing this, Avrohom declared, *"They merited to come out of the ark only because of the kindness they displayed towards the animals! I also will perform loving kindnesses — but with people."*

He began to do this, as it is said, "And he planted an *eshel* tree" — the individual letters of which signify in Hebrew "eating," "drinking," and "staying overnight", i.e., the three essential needs of a guest. Our Sages comment on this *midrash* that had Avrohom not conceived a jealousy of Shem, son of Noach, in the sphere of *chessed* performance, Avrohom's magnificent career in *chessed* would never have been initiated!

❖

Chapter 17

כעס

ANGER

We can all recognise easily enough the disadvantages of getting angry. In anger, we lose control of ourselves, and say and do things which we would never otherwise contemplate. Once our intellect has lost its grip on us, all types of transgressions, such as *loshon hora* and shaming one's fellow-man, may ensue. (Even a person who cannot be classed as an *angry person* but frequently gets vexed, comes into this category.)

Anger — a False Idol

Our Rabbis tell us that a person who becomes angry is considered an idol-worshipper. How can we understand this maxim? The answer is that one who cannot control himself will be liable to be cast about this way and that by his emotions and he may possibly eventually reach the very lowest level of idol-worship. Indeed this is the method of the *yetzer hora* which tells a person on one day, "Do this," and the next day commands him to transgress even further — thereby setting into motion a downward spiral.

Cure for Anger

Is there a cure for anger? We ought to examine several possible differing methods of dealing with this emotion.

(1) Recognising the triggers for anger and watching out for them.

(2) Thinking about the shame and emotional damage to oneself that anger often brings in its wake.

(3) Trying to engage in an occupation which does not arouse one to frequent anger and annoyance. (An angry person should not become a teacher.)

(4) Being aware that anger is not only a bad trait but also a grave transgression.

Common Causes of Anger

(1) A situation in which other people do not do what *you* wish them to.

(2) Someone downgrading your character.

(3) Feeling that someone has done something against you.

An example from everyday life: Someone hurts your feelings, but with a real effort of will you manage to hold in your sense of grievance. Then someone else does something much more slight against you. (This is really but a trifle compared to the previous event.) Suddenly all your pent-up anger spills out and you lash out at the person nearest to you, namely, the one who committed the second, less serious, offense.

Corrective Measures

(1) For Cause (1) (see above), one might proceed in the following way. Recognise that every individual has rights and that others do not necessarily have to accept *your* opinions or obey *your* wishes. Learn to have real respect for your friends' opinions. Also repeat over and over to yourself that anger is not really acceptable human behaviour, and truly decent individuals are not prone to it. Finally, think: what gives you the right to vent your anger against others?

(2) To guard against Causes (2) and (3) (see above), accustom yourself to the idea that people are *not* out to deliberately hurt and slight you. Allow a margin for error and always give the benefit of the doubt until the matter becomes clarified.

≪❖≫

CHAPTER 18

גאוה

PRIDE

What is pride? Pride is rooted in the individual's inherent feelings of his or her superiority over others. One can feel this superiority for a number of reasons: because of one's wisdom, beauty, good lineage (*yichus*), good character, wealth, and so on.

Pride is rooted in the heart, but it manifests itself in modes of speech, haughtiness, facial or hand movements, deportment, changes of expression.

Girls will often display their pride through sneering, disdainful comments or pointed jokes. (Such girls are usually despised by their friends even though they might appear to show respect to their faces!)

Yet, the Torah warns us explicitly against the quality of pride. In *Parshas Ekev*, we read: "Guard yourself, lest you forget the L-rd your G-d ... and your heart becomes proud ... and you say to yourself, 'My own strength and energy have gained me success' " (*Devorim* 8, 11-17).

How to Assess Whether One Is Free from Pride or Not

We find that there are some apparently very modest girls who feel themselves to be far from proud! But are they truly free from this most detrimental of qualities? Try this test. If you succeed in some project that all your friends have failed in, what do you feel, deep in your heart? Is there a tiny spark of joy or self-satisfaction in having succeeded *where others have failed*? If the answer is yes then you have not truly eradicated pride from your heart.

❖

CHAPTER 19

שנאה ונקמה

HATRED AND TAKING REVENGE

Hatred and taking revenge are the subject of a specific negative commandment in the Torah:

> *Do not hate your brother in your heart ... Do not take revenge or bear a grudge.*
> (*Vayikro* 19, 17-18)

There are several possible causes for hatred:

(1) A girl hates her friend because she has done her some wrong. She has put her to shame or spoken *loshon hora* against her.

(2) A girl harbours a grudge against her friend because she has not acceded to a particular request. Example: She would not agree to lend her a certain item or generally to help her in other ways.

Yet, even taking these facts into consideration hatred is absolutely forbidden.

Let us quote the Rambam:

> *It is forbidden for a man to be cruel, and refuse to be appeased. Rather he should be easily pacified and slow to anger, and when someone asks forgiveness he should forgive wholeheartedly and willingly. This is the way of the Jewish nation! Anger of idol-worshippers lasts forever.*
> (*Hilchos Teshuvo*, Chapter 2, *Halocho* 10)

Baseless Hatred

There is a certain type of hatred in which the object of this extreme emotion is totally free of guilt. He or she is hated by another without even having given provocation, the only cause being that he or she is cleverer or more popular, or possesses more personal charm or wealth, etc.

One must guard oneself against this all too common evil. We must free ourselves of this kind of *sinas chinom* so that we should be worthy to welcome *Moshiach*.

Taking Revenge and Bearing a Grudge

Hatred brings in its wake many related misdeeds, such as bearing a grudge and taking revenge. The prohibition of taking revenge applies even if, say, a girl has decided to withhold some benefit from her friend as a form of revenge, without actually damaging her or her property. But even if she does not go that far but simply reminds her of the wrong she has committed against her, she can still be guilty of transgressing the commandment, "Do not bear a grudge." (For example, if she says, "I have not forgotten what you did to me *x* weeks ago, but I am not like you — for in

THE JEWISH DAUGHTER

spite of this, I will still do you a favour.")[1] No, the Torah commands us to completely forget the misdeed and to act towards our friends as if they have never done us any wrong whatever. What is past is past and we are required to lay the past completely to rest. (For do *we* not enjoin the Almighty, in our prayers, to do just this for us?)

It is permissible for her to harbour grudges about her friend's behaviour only if she has done some real damage to her or spoilt her reputation. But once her friend has done all in her power to put right the wrong she did and asked to be forgiven for her misdeed by admitting what she did wrong, she must be willing to do so.

Acting Kindly towards Someone Who Hates Us

Even if it is absolutely obvious that a certain girl hates you (and she has actually harmed you several times), in spite of this you are dutybound to behave towards her with proper kindness, for example, to lend her money or articles. This is stated clearly in the text:

> *If you chance upon the ass of your enemy, collapsing under its burden, and the thought crosses your mind not to help him, you should suppress this feeling and on the contrary make doubly sure you assist him.*
>
> (*Shemos* 23, 5)

Further, our Sages teach us that if you chance across two animals — both struggling — one belonging to your friend and one to your enemy, you should help your enemy's ass first. This is because our natural instincts would tell us to do quite the opposite!

---

[1] See Rashi, *Parshas Kedoshim, Vayikro* 19, 18.

Post-Argument Strategies

Two girls who had a previous argument should not discuss their quarrel. This is because, in dissecting all the details, it is possible that they may start to quarrel again. Even if a proper argument does not ensue, there is bound to be unpleasantness and the renewed bond of friendship between them will be weakened.[2]

---

[2] According to *Orchos Tzaddikim*.

CHAPTER 20

גנות העזות

THE EVIL OF ARROGANCE

Arrogant ones are bound for Gehinom, bashful ones for Gan Eden.

(*Ovos* 5, 23)

Our Sages rarely make such a sharp and clear ruling concerning a character trait. The truth is that anyone who is proud and conceited is by definition not open to instruction from his parents, *Rabbonim*, or teachers! Moreover such a person will be involved in constant arguments, ending up by hating or putting others to shame. Since she is proud she will never admit that she is in the wrong, but will always seek self-justification! If pride will not allow one to accord respect even to one who is superior or greater, then it will certainly never permit one to treat one's colleagues with respect. Such a personality type always feels that justice is on his or her side! (Stubbornness is a quality closely related to pride.)

How Do We Set about Correcting Arrogance?

Chazal tell us that a person should take care to be:

> *As tender as a reed, and not rigid as a cedar tree.*
> (*Ta'anis* 20)

Consider this maxim well, for it implies that we should always be open to the opinions of others. Just as no two people are alike facially, no two people will hold exactly the same opinion! Be aware of this and be prepared to bend and adapt!

❖

Chapter 21

קמצנות ופזרנות

STINGINESS AND EXTRAVAGANCE

Stinginess and extravagance are two diametrically opposed qualities and both are undesirable!

Stinginess is in direct opposition to the distinguishing character of the Jewish nation as a whole. Our Sages state:

> There are three distinguishing marks of a Jew. A Jew is merciful, bashful, and generous.
> (*Yevomos* 79, 1)

The quality of kindness is bequeathed to us by Avrohom our forefather, as it is written:

> In order that he should command his sons and household after him, that they should observe the ways of Hashem, performing charity and justice.
> (*Bereshis* 18, 19)

One who cannot bear others to derive benefit from his or her wealth or possessions is far indeed from the spirit of Avrohom our forefather!

No one should conceive such a love of money that giving charity or entertaining guests actually hurts him or her. We are explicitly enjoined against possessing this type of feeling, as we are told:

> *You should surely give and not be aggrieved in your heart.*
>
> (*Devorim* 15, 10)

(However, we must be careful not to confuse stinginess with thriftiness, which is a good quality.)

We also come across personality types who are *stingy* with regard to their knowledge. They are unwilling to help others to progress because they feel that they might lose out.

Extravagance

Extravagance is also a trait to be eschewed at all costs! Here we must point out that extravagance is quite different from generosity. A generous person bases his actions on Torah and on Rabbinic sayings. The extravagant individual, however, acts without any sort of calculations.

Thriftiness

Before you buy anything costly, ask yourself the following questions: "Do I really need this? Can I perhaps find it cheaper elsewhere? Should I rather buy some other necessity, which is needed more urgently?"[1] Think about the fact that perhaps your parents (or your husband) are not wealthy enough to support all

---

[1] A famous Yiddish proverb states: "One who is a good housekeeper (*a gute balaboste*) is worth half a livelihood (*parnoso*)."

your extravagances! Also, ponder on whether or not you yourself were granted money for this particular purpose?

Wasting — בל תשחית

We have been instructed not to destroy anything that could be of possible use later. For example, the Torah commands us not to destroy fruit trees, for it is always possible to find other trees for timber. Even in wartime this commandment is still relevant. We are warned further not to *waste* unduly. We refer to this as *bal tashchis*.

Even when it comes to giving charity, we are told not to give away more than one fifth of one's wealth or of one's earnings, for one may perhaps incur poverty oneself.

We ought never to waste food, but instead appreciate its importance for mankind. We can perhaps learn this lesson from a well-known *minhag* which we have — covering the *challos* at *kiddush* time. This is because we wish not to "put the *challos* to shame," so to speak, when we say the blessing on the wine first (normally, the *berocho* would be said first on bread). Just think for a moment about this! If we are asked to take care not to shame certain foods, how much more ought we not to waste them!

≺≺❖≻≻

CHAPTER 22

לשון הרע ולשון נקי

LOSHON HORA, TALE-BEARING AND REFINEMENT IN SPEECH

The speaking of *loshon hora* is indicative of intrinsic bad qualities. For if we truly loved our fellow-man, we would have no desire at all to publicise his or her shortcomings.

With sufficient will power, one should be able to avoid *loshon hora*. The rewards are innumerable, as the Vilna Gaon writes in a well-known letter to his wife: "For every moment that a man closes his mouth and refrains from forbidden talk, he gains the *hidden light* which no angel can attain."

The Vilna Gaon writes further that the main thing to aim for is the avoidance of *loshon hora*, by not talking about anyone even in a praiseworthy way!

Judging Others Favourably — לדון לכף זכות

As a general rule, one should be dubious about the vast proportion of what is said in conversation, for without knowledge of all the relevant details, the tenor of what one hears can be

THE JEWISH DAUGHTER

completely changed. The object of the *loshon hora* might have not meant badly, or might perhaps have come to regret his or her actions afterwards.

Curiosity

This is a source of great temptation to most women. Nevertheless, with effort curiosity *can* be controlled. This is especially true in a case where one knows that the other party wishes to keep her secret or she suspects that if it were to come out some form of harm, damage, or embarrassment might result.

Secrets — לשמור סוד

There is an outright prohibition against revealing a secret, as is stated in the text:

> *He who goes as a tale-bearer will reveal secrets.*
> (Mishlei 11, 13)

By natural inclination we know that it is often difficult for a woman to keep a secret and if she is told something by a friend she may find it tempting to reveal it. It is therefore preferable to be reluctant to share other people's secrets and matters of extreme importance.

These are the words of the Chofetz Chaim on secrets:

> *A person must keep in confidence a secret which his or her friend has told him or her — even if there is no question of tale-bearing, in revealing it. For in its revelation one displays a disregard for the secret-holder, which breaks the bounds of modesty.*

(In *Be'er Mayim Chaim*, the Chofetz Chaim states that transgressing this matter is more severe than *loshon hora* and its offshoots.)

Refinement in Speech

Our Rabbis frequently and strongly stress the need for refinement in speech. Rabbi Yehoshua ben Levi states:

> *Never allow yourself to use a despicable form of language.*
>
> (*Pesochim* 3, 1)

For example: If there is an unpleasant smell, it is possible to say there is a smell which is "not nice," or better still, not to comment at all. Other people also have noses!

Even words in the dictionary such as *pig* should not be used with reference to an individual (or one's children). The Chazon Ish would not allow anyone in his presence to call another person a *liar*. One would have to say that such-and-such a person is liable not to always speak the truth!

One should try to always look for the positive and pleasant aspects in all things. This is illustrated in the following anecdote:

Two people were once walking past a dead lion. One of them remarked, "What a bad smell!" The other commented, "Yes, that is true, but look at his beautiful teeth."

❖

Chapter 23

לימוד תורה

TORAH STUDY

A man's extensive comprehensive obligations in the sphere of Torah study are codified in the Rambam. A woman, on the other hand, is required to study only those *halochos* which pertain specifically to her. These are fairly numerous and include: the laws of prayer, washing hands for a meal, laws of meat and milk, checking for worms, laws of *loshon hora*, *berochos*, *Shabbos*, and *Yom Tov*. If she is in business she must take great care in the laws relating to commercial practice. These are but a few examples.

In addition to the above, she must attempt to strengthen her *emuno*, spiritual outlook, and *yiras Shomayim* by acquainting herself with sources — such as *Chumosh*, *Midrash*, history from the creation of the world to *Matan Torah*, and Jewish history from the Exodus to the *Churbon*.[1]

---

[1] In former times many books were written for women, for example, the *Tzena Urena* in Yiddish. The Vilna Gaon also writes in his famous letter which he sent to his wife, on his journey to Eretz Yisroel (which was never completed): "Amongst my *seforim* there is *Mishlei* in Yiddish and it is far better to read this daily than other words of *Mussar*. You should also read *Koheles* on a regular basis."

The Importance of *Limmud Torah* for Men

It is extremely important for a Jewish girl to recognise *the value* of *limmud Torah* for men. We can derive an inkling of the true significance of Torah study from the text itself:

> *The Torah of Hashem is pure, reviving the soul. It is pleasanter than gold and fine gold and sweeter than honey.*
>
> (*Tehillim* 19)

> *How I love your Torah. Every day it forms the subject of my conversation!*
>
> (*Tehillim* 119)

> *It is more precious than a diamond and all material possessions cannot be equalled to it. Length of days is in its right hand, and in its left wealth and honour. Its ways are paths of pleasantness, and all its paths are peaceful. It is a tree of life to all those who grasp it and those that uphold it are happy.*
>
> (*Mishlei* 3, 15-18)

Thus says Rabbi Nehoray (that is Rabbi Meir):

> *I have set aside all the professions that exist in the world, and I have taught my son nothing but Torah. For a man gains a reward for Torah in this world, and a portion in the World to Come. Torah is his protection from evil in his youth and offers him hope in his old age.*[2]

---

[2] *Kiddushin* 82.

The *Torah* Learned by Children

Our Sages stated that the Torah learned by children takes precedence over even building the *Bais Hamikdosh* (*Shabbos* 119, 2). Their Torah has a special preciousness for the Almighty. This is because the speech of children is totally pure and innocent.

Bitul Torah — ביטול תורה

The concept of *bitul Torah*, i.e., not to miss any opportunity for learning Torah and not to disturb a person when he is learning Torah, may seem foreign to a girl, who is not bound by this prohibition herself. But she should be aware that a man is required to offer an accounting for each moment and how it has been used in the service of G-d.

Our Sages stated:

> *Torah study is great, for without it the heavens and earth would not continue to exist.*[3] *"Thus said the Almighty — If not for My covenant day and night (the continuous study of Torah) the laws governing heaven and earth would not function.*
> (*Yirmeyohu* 33, 25)

This means that Torah study maintains the world in an absolute sense. This concept is explained in the *sefer Nefesh Hachayim*[4] where we are told that should Torah study cease G-d forbid, altogether for one moment only, the world would revert to chaos and confusion!

---

[3] *Nedorim* 32.
[4] *Shaar* 4, Chapter 11.

We can see therefore that the Torah study of each and every individual has within itself the ability to maintain the world. We know that great Torah Sages would be particular to study Torah in the hours immediately following Yom Kippur, when everyone else naturally hurries to eat — for they feared that Torah study might cease altogether at that moment!

Disturbing the Study of Torah

It constitutes a serious transgression to disturb any individual from the study of Torah, even for only a moment, for we cannot measure the greatness of the corrective potential of one tiny second of Torah study in the world! Therefore before you call someone away from his Torah learning, stop and think — is it really urgent, or can it wait perhaps until he has finished learning?

Any woman who has acquired a deep knowledge and love of Torah will know automatically how best to assist her husband in this sphere. She will try not to burden him with requests that distract him unduly. She alone has the power of protecting his learning and that of her children, and this is a not inconsiderable role!

Respect for *Torah* — כבוד התורה

It is a great *mitzvo* to accord respect to *talmidei chachomim* (Torah scholars). It is written in the Torah:

> *Stand up before an old man and offer respect for the zoken (lit., aged one).*
>
> (*Vayikro* 19, 32)

The word *zoken* refers to one who is in possession of Torah wisdom. One is duty bound then to accord *zekenim* all types of honour: to stand up when they enter a room, to place them at the head of any gathering, not to contradict their words, etc. This includes not merely *gedolei Yisroel* (Torah giants) but anyone who is a *talmid chochom*, be he a *Rov* of a community, *Dayan*, *Rosh Yeshivo*, or a learned man.[5]

◄◄❖►►

---

[5] The Rambam states in his *Hilchos Talmud Torah* (1.1): "One is obliged to honour any *talmid chochom*, even if he is not one's *Rebbe*."

Chapter 24

תשובה

THE POWER OF REPENTANCE

One of the most singular kindnesses which *Hashem* has dealt us is allowing us the opportunity for repentance. Whether we have sinned but once or on numerous occasions, the gates of repentance are always open to us.

The Almighty is like a merciful father who eagerly awaits our turning to Him in repentance, as it is written:

> *Return, wayward children, I will cure you of your sins.*
>
> (*Yirmeyohu* 3, 22)

Fortunate is she who achieves true repentance, for G-d will forgive all her sins. She is granted the opportunity to return to her pre-sinful state. The Rambam elucidates this point for us. "Yesterday," he states, "this same person was hated by the Almighty, despised, cast out at a distance, regarded as an abomination. Today, after his repentance, he is as close to His Creator as a beloved son" (*Hilchos Teshuvo*, Chapter 7). The possibilities for *teshuvo* are not limited to the month of *Ellul* or the Ten Days of Penitence. No, it is an option open to any individual who has committed a sin, either erroneously or through the persuasion or pressure of friends. The quicker one experiences remorse for one's actions and repents, the better!

What are the commonest areas of sin? Moving *muktzo* objects or performing *melochos* on *Shabbos* due to ignorance of the *halocho*, neglecting to perform the *mitzvo* of honouring one's father and mother, speaking *loshon hora*, saying a *berocho* in vain in error, neglecting to say an *after berocho* due to forgetfulness, carrying out business dealings in a fraudulent manner, giving way to anger, lying, using the object of another person without permission, etc.

However, any individual who has sinned should not fall into the trap of despair. This is a grave mistake! Of course, regret is appropriate. But despair in any shape or form, no! We can distinguish between regret, which can be positive and lead to *teshuvo,* and despair, on the other hand, which is a totally negative emotion.

What constitutes regret?

An individual should feel deeply sorry for what he or she has done and wish sincerely that such an action had never been committed. Such feelings are a source of *teshuvo*! Even if after experiencing feelings of regret, she falls again into the trap of performing this self-same deed, there is nothing to stop her from entering the cycle of regret again but with greater force and commitment. Even if she sins several times, regret is still possible, for one does not win a war with one battle! Perseverance will ultimately lead to a full repentance, and all the rewards which this entails.

The Mechanism of Repentance — תשובה

Our Sages outlined four principle roads to repentance:

(1) Abandoning one's sin — עזיבת החטא.

(2) Regret — חרטה.

(3) A sincere and genuine undertaking not to sin — קבלה להבא.

(4) Confession before G-d — וודוי.

We can see that a heartfelt regret must be coupled with the practical action of abandoning one's sin. "I have sinned ... and I regret this. I will not return to my foolishness again." These are the emotions one should feel.

Once a full repentance has been achieved, the individual should feel that the slate has been wiped clean. One stands before G-d as pure as on the day of one's birth![1]

≺≺❖≻≻

---

[1] This Chapter is based on *Rabbenu* Yonah, in his *Shaarei Teshuvo* and on the Rambam, *Hilchos Teshuvo*. For more detail, see *The Practical Guide to Teshuvo* by the author.

חלק ההלכה

Laws of *Tznius* and *Yichud*

Chapter 25

Tznius In Halocho

The underlying purpose of the general laws of *tznius* is twofold:

(1) To raise the level of social behaviour and general conduct of man and woman alike.

(2) To delineate certain limits in the sphere of the appearance of women.

In this book we are dealing with the *tznius* of the woman.

Dress

A woman should take care not to reveal even the slightest parts of her body and legs.[1] She should ensure that her dress or garment rises up to the neck, both from the front and back. It is permissible to bare the neck itself. The sleeves should cover the

---

[1] There are two prohibitions here, both of which originate from the Torah: (1) immodesty; (2) not putting a stumbling-block before men.
Any part of the body which is normally covered is considered *ervo*. This must not be judged by present day standards, but rather on the standards of *tznius* which Jewish girls were accustomed to have.

elbows at the least.² The length of the skirt or dress should allow for adequate covering of the knees even in the sitting position (and even if one wears tights full-length).

The legs must be covered in *opaque* tights. There are some materials which are not normally transparent but in the sunlight reveal the contours of the body and legs. In a wide garment such as a smock this problem is more common (and one should be aware of it as many people fall into this trap through lack of awareness).

One should not tend towards leniency in the sphere of these *halochos* even in an age or locality where they are contrary to accepted practice. Where the *minhag* of the place is to cover parts of the body which the *halocho* does not specify, the *minhag* should assume the stringency of a *din*.

We should mention here the prohibition:

> *A man's garments should not be worn by a woman, nor a woman's garments by a man, for it is an abomination to G-d.*
>
> (Devorim 22, 5)

Note: This prohibition applies even when the fashion is that women's clothing resembles that of men (e.g., the wearing of trousers).³

Swimming

It is permissible for a girl or woman to swim in the sea or to sun-bathe, but only on a secluded separate women's beach, or in a

---

² According to the *Mishna Berura*, Chapter 75, sub-paragraph 2.
³ On the subject of women wearing trousers, see *Minchas Yitzchok*, Part 2, 108, and *Igros Moshe, Yoreh Deoh* 1, Chapter 81.

THE JEWISH DAUGHTER

swimming pool at a time set aside for women only.[4]

It is forbidden for men, teenaged boys, or even younger boys to go to mixed swimming.[5]

Exercising in Front of Men

It is forbidden for a woman to exercise in front of men if she is not dressed in accordance with the *Halocho*.

It is against the spirit of *tznius* to do so even if she *is* properly dressed. This applies also to dancing at a *chasuno* in front of men.

Hair Covering

Married women, widows, or divorced women, *must* cover their hair completely when leaving the house[6] or in front of men, but it is the accepted custom to cover one's hair *in the house* even in the circle of one's own family. The *minhag* is to wear a wig (*shaitel*). Those who are stricter wear other forms of covering.[7]

Our Rabbis teach us that the purity of one's children's souls is dependent on this great quality of *tznius* with regard to hair covering, even in a woman's house where no one sees her (except when she washes, etc.) Obviously this applies also to her conduct of *tznius* generally.

---

[4] See 1. It seems that if the pool is specified for the use of women, one need not prohibit this although sometimes male pool attendants are present. (There might be a consideration of *tznius*, but not as a matter of law.) A Jewish attendant *is* prohibited to enter therein.
[5] The *issur* of looking at parts of the body which are normally covered applies here.
[6] *Even Ho'ezer*, Chapter 21, 2, and Chapter 115, 4. This is a Torah prohibition, as is written in *Kesubos* 72.
[7] *Orach Chayim*, Chapter 75, בבאור הלכה ד"ה ודע.

Not Completely Dressed

It is forbidden to undress completely - even for a moment - in a room containing *seforim*. It is permissible to undress if the books are covered.

It is permissible for a woman to make a blessing when she is not completely dressed and also in front of women who are not completely dressed.[8]

It is a modest form of behaviour not to uncover parts of the body which are normally kept hidden, needlessly, even when one is alone in a room. Even when changing, one should be aware of this point, wherever possible.[9]

Singing

It is forbidden for girls from the age of twelve upwards to sing in front of men and it is forbidden for men to listen to their singing.[10] It is against the spirit of *tznius* to do so even below that age (unless the girl is very young). Some authorities are lenient with regard to singing within the family circle: in front of a father, grandfather, son, or brother. Some authorities are stricter in forbidding singing in front of a brother (it all depends upon one's custom).

A husband is allowed to listen to his wife's singing when she is *pure*, but not when he is praying or learning.

◄◄❖►►

---

[8] *Orach Chayim*, Chapter 75, 1.
[9] As is related in *Maseches Yoma* 47: "Kimchis bore seven sons who became High Priests due to her merit of never letting the ceiling see the hair of her head."
[10] The voice of a woman is counted like an *ervo* for a man, and is forbidden even at times other than Torah study or prayer. Young girls from about the age of twelve are all considered *niddo* by law (*Mishna Berura*, Chapter 75, 17) and it is forbidden for men to hear them singing.

CHAPTER 26

הלכות יחוד

THE PROHIBITION OF YICHUD

Definition

It is forbidden for a woman, single or married, to enter into seclusion with a man, be he single or married, even for a short while.[1] The purpose of this *din* is to erect a barrier against transgression. This applies to places where there is no likelihood that they will be disturbed by others. For example, a house locked from within, a flat or room locked with a key, or a secluded spot, whether in a city centre or in a field or park. The concept of "in seclusion" (יחוד) in relation to this *halocho* is relative. Sometimes it includes situations in which other people are present, if their presence will not prevent sin.

With Whom

It is forbidden for a girl of twelve upwards, or for a woman, to be alone with:

---

[1] The laws of *yichud* are based principally on *Shulchon Oruch*, *Even Ho'ezer*, Chapter 22.

(1) A boy — Jew or non-Jew — from the age of nine upwards,[2] for example, a babysitter or a cousin.

(2) A man — Jew or non-Jew, married or single — even if he is her fiancé (she is engaged to him) or even if he is a relative.

Exceptions to this rule are:
a father, grandfather, son, grandson, or brother.

Adopted Children or Stepchildren

The prohibition of *yichud* applies to adoptive parents, because there is no blood-relationship between them and their adopted children.

Brother and Sister

There is no prohibition of *yichud* for a brother and sister, but it is forbidden for them to live in a flat alone for more than thirty days, and according to stricter authorities, for more that seven days.[3] This does not apply to brothers and sisters who have no blood relationship between them, such as step- or adopted children.

Example: The children of a couple who are married for the second time, and each one has children from the former marriage.

The Influence of Age or State of Health

The prohibition of *yichud* applies even to the ill, incapacitated, or the old, even at an advanced age.

---

[2] The subject of whether the prohibition of *yichud* applies to a minor (boy or girl), from the viewpoint of *chinuch*, is dealt with in *Devar Halocho*, Chapter 3.

[3] עי' חלקת מחוקק סי' כ"ב ס"ק א' וב"ש שם דיחוד מותר באח ואחות לפרקים. ושעור פרקים י"א ל' יום וי"א ז' ימים.

Places Where *Yichud* Applies

The *issur* (prohibition) of *yichud* applies in a room or house where it is not likely that strangers will enter. Practical examples:

- A man and woman living in separate rooms in the same house.

- A man and woman who are alone in a room locked from within, e.g., an office or a room which people do not generally enter (even if not locked), like a cellar or a disused attic room, even if there are others in the house.

- A woman visiting a doctor's office, if the door is locked or when there are no other people in the building.

- An employer and his worker or workers.

    A man and a woman who work together in a locked office or an office not frequented by other people, such as a principal and his secretary.

- A business-woman who sees sales representatives or clients at home, if the door is locked. (It is permissible if her husband is in the same city.)

- A sales woman who sees clients in their own homes.

- Workmen who work in the house of a woman who lives alone.

- Girls who take music lessons with a male teacher or vice-versa.

Secluded Places

The *issur* of *yichud* applies to isolated places such as a forest, field, secluded beach, or country lane.

It is not right for a fiancé to walk with his bride in isolated places or even in parts of a city where it is known that there is normally no one around at that hour of the day or night.

Ways in Which *Yichud* May Be Allowed

- ### The Door of the House Is Open — פתח פתוח לרשות הרבים

    There is no *issur* of *yichud* in a place where another person is likely to enter suddenly. Therefore, there is no prohibition of *yichud* during the day and in the early hours of the evening, if the doors of the house or apartment, and the room, are not locked. If the street is deserted, even at these hours, it is forbidden to enter into *yichud*. Even when *yichud* is allowed, it is preferable to leave the doors slightly ajar.

    There is no prohibition of *yichud* when the door is locked if there are other key holders who are in a position to open the door and enter at will at any time. However, if one imposes limitations so that this person cannot use the key at will or if he is hesitant to enter for any reason, *yichud* does apply — for example, during the night, when the holder of the key would not be welcome.

- ### If the Wife Is at Home — האשה בבית

    If a girl or a woman stays overnight in a Jewish house where there is only the husband and his wife, there is no question of *yichud*. But it is forbidden for a Jewish girl or woman to stay overnight in a non-Jewish home even when the wife is at home. During the day it would be necessary to leave the door open if she is in the house.[4]

A Single Woman

A girl or a woman living alone should be careful concerning the *issur* of *yichud* whenever a man — Jew or non-Jew — enters the house. The prohibition applies even to relations, for example, her father-in-law, brother-in-law, or her nephew. She is allowed to be alone with her father, son, grandfather, grandson, or brother. (A brother can reside in his sister's house for thirty days maximum.) There is no prohibition of *yichud* if there are people in the street and the door of the house is open or unlocked, or in other words, it is possible to enter from without. It is possible also to give a key to a neighbour or relation (it is preferable to give it to two people) and to give them permission to enter at any time (and they should actually do this sometimes) to remove the threat of *yichud*. The giving of a key allows the prohibition of *yichud* to be waived only during the day or the early hours of the evening.

A Man and His Relatives

If the mother, grandmother, sister, daughter, or granddaughter of a man living alone are in the house, there are those who permit the presence of another woman (such a relation may act as *shomeres*). In this instance one should consult a *Rov*. (If two women are blood relations, such as sisters, a mother and daughter,

---

[4] It is surprising how accepted is the practice amongst some Orthodox families of sending their daughter to a non-Jewish male teacher to perfect herself in some area, e.g., music, and the door of the house in which she studies may be locked. We know that even if the wife of the teacher is present, this is not permissible.

a niece and aunt, the prohibition of *yichud* remains in force, when they visit one a man lives alone.[5]

This chapter is only a general guide to the laws of *yichud*. The subject of *yichud* is dealt with in more detail in the booklet "*Taharas Am Yisroel* (I)".[6]

≺≺❖≻≻

---

[5] On the subject of whether a mother, daughter, or sister is considered a valid *shomeres*, the *Pis'che Teshuvo* says that this is not permitted. See also *sefer Taharas Yisroel*, laws of *yichud*, *Be'er Yitzchok* 25-26, but there are many *Acharonim* who rule leniently in this matter. In an emergency one can possibly be lenient, because in the final analysis, when there are more than two people present it does not constitute *yichud* as prohibited by the Torah. (If it is a Rabbinical prohibition, we may be more lenient.) In all instances one should ask a *sh'ailo*.

There is no *issur* of *yichud* when a woman and her mother-in-law are present or two sisters-in-law, for these women will not cover up one for the other, and therefore act as a deterrent to sin. This applies to daylight hours, but by night two *shomrim* are required.

[6] To be called in future editions "*Kedushas Am Yisroel*".